G000167973

by Iain Gray

Lang**Syne**

PUBLISHING

WRITING *to* REMEMBER

Lang**Syne**

PUBLISHING

WRITING *to* REMEMBER

79 Main Street, Newtongrange,
Midlothian EH22 4NA
Tel: 0131 344 0414   Fax: 0845 075 6085
E-mail: info@lang-syne.co.uk
www.langsyneshop.co.uk

Design by Dorothy Meikle
Printed by Ricoh Print Scotland
© Lang Syne Publishers Ltd 2015

ISBN 978-1-85217-215-2

King

Echoes of a far distant past
can still be found in most names

Chapter one:

Origins of Scottish surnames

by George Forbes

It all began with the Normans.

For it was they who introduced surnames into common usage more than a thousand years ago, initially based on the title of their estates, local villages and chateaux in France to distinguish and identify these landholdings, usually acquired at the point of a bloodstained sword.

Such grand descriptions also helped enhance the prestige of these arrogant warlords and generally glorify their lofty positions high above the humble serfs slaving away below in the pecking order who only had single names, often with Biblical connotations as in Pierre and Jacques.

The only descriptive distinctions among this peasantry concerned their occupations, like Pierre the swineherd or Jacques the ferryman.

The Normans themselves were originally Vikings (or Northmen) who raided, colonised and eventually settled down around the French coastline.

They had sailed up the Seine in their long-boats in 900AD under their ferocious leader Rollo and ruled the roost in north east France before sailing over to conquer England, bringing their relatively new tradition of having surnames with them.

It took another hundred years for the Normans to percolate northwards and surnames did not begin to appear in Scotland until the thirteenth century.

These adventurous knights brought an aura of chivalry with them and it was said no damsel of any distinction would marry a man unless he had at least two names.

The family names included that of Scotland's great hero Robert De Brus and his compatriots were warriors from families like the De Morevils, De Umphravils, De Berkelais, De Quincis, De Viponts and De Vaux.

As the knights settled the boundaries of

their vast estates, they took territorial names, as in Hamilton, Moray, Crawford, Cunningham, Dunbar, Ross, Wemyss, Dundas, Galloway, Renfrew, Greenhill, Hazelwood, Sandylands and Church-hill.

Other names, though not with any obvious geographical or topographical features, nevertheless derived from ancient parishes like Douglas, Forbes, Dalyell and Guthrie.

Other surnames were coined in connection with occupations, castles or legendary deeds. Stuart originated in the word steward, a prestigious post which was an integral part of any large medieval household. The same applied to Cooks, Chamberlains, Constables and Porters.

Borders towns and forts – needed in areas like the Debateable Lands which were constantly fought over by feuding local families – had their own distinctive names; and it was often from them that the resident groups took their communal titles, as in the Grahams of Annandale, the Elliots and Armstrongs of the East Marches, the Scotts and Kerrs of Teviotdale and Eskdale.

Even physical attributes crept into surnames, as in Small, Little and More (the latter being 'beg' in Gaelic), Long or Lang, Stark, Stout, Strong or Strang and even Jolly.

Mieklejohns would have had the strength of several men, while Littlejohn was named after the legendary sidekick of Robin Hood.

Colours got into the act with Black, White, Grey, Brown and Green (Red developed into Reid, Ruddy or Ruddiman). Blue was rare and nobody ever wanted to be associated with yellow.

Pompous worthies took the name Wiseman, Goodman and Goodall.

Words intimating the sons of leading figures were soon affiliated into the language as in Johnson, Adamson, Richardson and Thomson, while the Norman equivalent of Fitz (from the French-Latin 'filius' meaning 'son') cropped up in Fitzmaurice and Fitzgerald.

The prefix 'Mac' was 'son of' in Gaelic and clans often originated with occupations – as in MacNab being sons of the Abbot, MacPherson and MacVicar being sons of the minister and MacIntosh being sons of the chief.

The church's influence could be found in the names Kirk, Clerk, Clarke, Bishop, Friar and Monk. Proctor came from a church official, Singer and Sangster from choristers, Gilchrist and Gillies from Christ's servant, Mitchell, Gilmory and Gilmour from servants of St Michael and Mary, Malcolm from a servant of Columba and Gillespie from a bishop's servant.

The rudimentary medical profession was represented by Barber (a trade which also once included dentistry and surgery) as well as Leech or Leitch.

Businessmen produced Merchants, Mercers, Monypennies, Chapmans, Sellers and Scales, while down at the old village watermill the names that cropped up included Miller, Walker and Fuller.

Other self explanatory trades included Coopers, Brands, Barkers, Tanners, Skinners, Brewsters and Brewers, Tailors, Saddlers, Wrights, Cartwrights, Smiths, Harpers, Joiners, Sawyers, Masons and Plumbers.

Even the scenery was utilised as in Craig, Moor, Hill, Glen, Wood and Forrest.

Rank, whether high or low, took its place with Laird, Barron, Knight, Tennant, Farmer, Husband, Granger, Grieve, Shepherd, Shearer and Fletcher.

The hunt and the chase supplied Hunter, Falconer, Fowler, Fox, Forrester, Archer and Spearman.

The renowned medieval historian Froissart, who eulogised about the romantic deeds of chivalry (and who condemned Scotland as being a poverty stricken wasteland), once sniffily dismissed the peasantry of his native France as the jacquerie (or the jacques-without-names) but it was these same humble folk who ended up over-throwing the arrogant aristocracy.

In the olden days, only the blueblooded knights of antiquity were entitled to full, proper names, both Christian and surnames, but with the passing of time and a more egalitarian, less feudal atmosphere, more respectful and worthy titles spread throughout the populace as a whole.

Echoes of a far distant past can still be found in most names and they can be borne with pride in commemoration of past generations who fought and toiled in some capacity or other to make our nation what it now is, for good or ill.

Chapter two:

Of royal race

The many thousands of Kings scattered across the world will be pleasantly surprised to learn that their proud surname may well indicate that royal blood flows through their veins, albeit in a rather diluted form today.

There are numerous points of origin of the name, but it is in Scotland that much of the romance and drama associated with it are to be found.

A Latin charter records a Robertus King living in the Garioch area of Aberdeenshire in the mid thirteenth century, but the name had been commonplace for some time before that.

Some sources state that 'King' may have been the name adopted by those who played the role of a king in the highly popular medieval pageants, or open-air plays, but this does not explain the proliferation of the surname.

Other sources assert it was a nickname for

someone who either had pretensions to royalty or disported themselves in a particularly haughty manner, but there may have been some basis for these pretensions.

It was not until about 843 A.D. that the separate kingdoms that now make up modern day Scotland were united under King Kenneth MacAlpin.

The west was the domain of the Scots, who had come to the mainland in about 500 A.D. from Ireland, and who eventually gave their name to the nation of Scotland, while Britons held the vast territory in the south known as Strathclyde.

Two separate tribes of Picts, probably the original native inhabitants of the land, were settled in the north and northeast, and all these separate kingdoms had their own chief, or king.

These kings were known in Gaelic as 'righ', and when an overall chief, or king, was appointed over them he was known as the 'Ard-Righ', or 'High King.'

As the power and control of a central monarchy gradually asserted itself, many of these lesser 'righ', or sub-kings, found their own power diminished.

From kings in their own right, many became mere subjects of the High King, retaining their lands and property in return for military service.

Many, however, found themselves dispossessed of their ancient rights in favour of others considered more loyal to the central monarchy.

Proud traditions die hard, however, and descendants of many of these former 'righ' retained a memory of their once glorious past by adopting the English form of 'King' as a surname.

It would be a near impossible task for Kings of today to trace a descent back to these early 'righ', or kings, but it may well be possible for those of a Scottish descent to trace a descent back to one particular Highland clan that claims a proud royal lineage.

This is the Clan MacGregor, or Clan Gregor, whose motto is 'S'rioghal mo dhream' ('royal is my race'), and whose crest is a lion's head crowned with an antique crown.

Claiming an ancient descent from Griogar, or Gregor, a son of Alpin, who was a king of Dalriada, the clan was destined to suffer terribly in subsequent centuries with even its proud name proscribed, or banned.

Many MacGregors, for their own safety, were forced to assume new identities by adopting new names, such as King.

These aliases were among a host of others adopted by the clan, and the official Clan Gregor Society, founded in 1822 and one of the oldest clan societies, lists 'King' among the forty-seven accepted MacGregor names and septs.

Only Kings of today who can trace a connection back to the ancient MacGregor homelands may be entitled to share in the clan's heritage and traditions.

As a sept, or branch, of the MacGregors, the history of the Kings is inextricably linked with that of the clan.

The western borders of Perthshire and the eastern borders of Argyll had, from what appears to have been time immemorial, been the hauntingly beautiful homelands of Clan Gregor.

These lands included Glengyle, Glenlyon, and Glenstrae, but, in a pattern that was to become all too familiar to the MacGregors and other smaller clans over a number of centuries, the powerful Clan Campbell steadily encroached on these lands.

This process started after Neil Campbell was granted the barony of Lochawe, at the expense of the MacGregors, for his loyal and faithful service to Robert the Bruce.

The MacGregors gradually found themselves in the humiliating role of mere tenants on what had for centuries been their own lands, a situation against which their defiant spirit soon rebelled, and they found an outlet for their passions by preying on their rather more law-abiding neighbours.

The MacGregors, inevitably, soon became victims of attempts by successive monarchs to impose law and order.

On two occasions during the reign of Mary, Queen of Scots, what were known as commissions of fire and sword were issued to clan chiefs who were victims of MacGregor raiding and pillaging.

This gave them virtual carte blanche to kill any MacGregor on sight and impound or destroy their property.

James VI resolved to make an example of the troublesome MacGregors once and for all, describing them as 'the wicked and unhappy race of the Clan Gregor', and determining to 'pursue and prosecute them with all rigour and extremity.'

An indication of the monarch's attitude towards his unruly subjects in general can be gleaned from his infamous statement that 'as for the Highlanders, I shortly comprehend them all in two sorts of people: the one that dwelleth in our main land, that are barbarous for the most part, are yet mixed with some civility: the other, that dwelleth in the isles, that are utterly barbarous, without any show of civility.'

Matters came to a bloody head for the MacGregors in February of 1603, when they met the Colquhouns of Luss in battle at Glenfruin, near Loch Lomond.

Subsequent accounts of the MacGregors' actions on the day were grossly exaggerated, but they did indeed kill at least sixty Colquhouns, including the laird of Luss, before ravaging their lands and making off with a rich booty of cattle, sheep, goats, and horses.

Hysterical reports, totally unfounded, also

claimed they had murdered a number of prisoners and a number of schoolboys from nearby Dumbarton.

The hysteria against the clan was further fuelled when a procession of the wives of the Colquhoun victims paraded through Edinburgh bearing their husbands' torn and bloody shirts.

An incensed James VI immediately arranged for the passing of an Act of Council, that imposed severe sanctions on the clan: these measures included the proscription, or banning, of the very name 'MacGregor' itself.

MacGregor of Glenstrae, the clan chief, was hanged along with eleven of his leading men at the Mercat Cross in Edinburgh, while a price of £1000 was put on the heads of other prominent members of the clan.

A lower sum was put on the heads of other MacGregors, and any clansman who brought in the head of one of his kinsmen was to be granted a full pardon: an option that very few, if any, MacGregor clansmen chose to exercise.

Another commission was granted eight

years later to 'root out and extirpate' the MacGregors, while in the seventeenth century equivalent of an act of ethnic cleansing, arrangements were made to forcibly remove MacGregor women and children to the Lowlands, while the women were branded on the face with a red-hot key.

MacGregors were also forbidden to carry any weapons, apart from a pointless knife to cut their meat, and no more than four were allowed to gather together at any one time.

These harsh measures were re-enacted in 1617 and 1635, rescinded for a time on the Restoration to the throne of Charles II in 1660, but restored again in 1693.

It was not until 1774 that the proscription on the name MacGregor was at last lifted and, while many who had been forced to adopt new names reverted back to MacGregor, others who had chosen aliases such as King retained this new name.

Chapter three:

For the Stuart cause

While the MacGregors had been perceived as a threat to established law and order, they also fought gallantly in the cause of Scotland's freedom.

Alistair MacGregor of Glenstrae, for example, was among the 3,000 clansmen who formed part of the 35,000-strong Scots army that met a strategically superior English force at the battle of Pinkie, near Musselburgh, on Scotland's east coast, in September of 1547.

Fought during the infancy of the ill-starred Mary, Queen of Scots, the battle resulted in a resounding victory for the English invasion force, despite the determination and bravery of clansmen such as the MacGregors.

In later years, the MacGregors also found themselves at the heart of the divisive wars between Crown and Covenant.

A National Covenant had first been

signed in the Greyfriars kirkyard, in Edinburgh, in February of 1638, pledging defence of the Presbyterian religion and defiance of Charles I's claim of supremacy in matters of religion.

Copies of the Covenant were circulated throughout the length and breadth of Scotland, and those who subscribed to it were known as Covenanters.

In the bitter civil war that followed the signing of the Covenant, the MacGregors fought at the side of the Royalist John Graham, 1st Marquis of Montrose, during his campaigns in support of the king and in opposition to the Covenanters.

The period from 1644-45 became known as the Year of Miracles because of Montrose's brilliant military successes.

These included the battle of Inverlochy, fought on February 2, 1645, when the Covenanting leader, the Earl of Argyll, was forced to flee to safety in his galley after 1,500 of his Covenanters were wiped out in a daring surprise attack.

What made Montrose's victory all the more remarkable was that his hardy band of men, including a contingent of MacGregors, had arrived at Inverlochy after enduring a gruelling thirty-six hour march through knee-deep snow from the area of present-day Fort Augustus to Inverlochy.

The MacGregors also shared in Montrose's victory at Kilsyth on August 15, 1645, but also shared in his final defeat at Philiphaugh, near Selkirk, less than a month later.

In the following century, the MacGregors would also share in the failures of both the 1715 and 1745 Jacobite Risings, the doomed attempts to restore the exiled Royal House of Stuart to the throne.

Included in the Jacobite ranks were also those MacGregors who had been forced to adopt a new surname, such as King.

It was the novelist Sir Walter Scott who romanticised and immortalised Rob Roy MacGregor, arguably the clan's most famous son.

Forced to assume his mother's surname of

Campbell because of the proscription on the MacGregor name, Rob Roy led not only a precarious existence as a freebooter, but contributed to the cause of the exiled Royal House of Stuart through his support of James III, known to posterity as the Old Pretender, in the Jacobite Rising of 1715.

Jacobite opposition to the succession to the throne in 1714 of George, the Elector of Hanover, reached such a pitch that on September 6 of the following year the Earl of Mar raised the Stuart Standard at Braemar.

He managed to muster a force of no less than 10,000 fighting men, including Rob Roy and his fellow clansmen, but the Jacobite cause was effectively lost after the battle of Sheriffmuir, in November of 1715, when Mar withdrew his forces north to Perth.

James landed at Peterhead from France in December, and then moved on to Perth, only to depart forever from Scottish shores in February of 1716.

The Rising had fizzled out, but the Stuart

Standard was raised again more than thirty years later when James's son, Prince Charles Edward Stuart, arrived on Scottish soil in July of 1745.

Rallying loyal support, a great victory followed at the battle of Prestonpans in September, and a confident Jacobite army left Edinburgh for the march on London at the end of October, only to controversially retire back north in early December after reaching Derby.

Clansmen such as the MacGregors rallied to the cause, under the leadership of John MacGregor of Glengyle, Evan MacGregor of Glencarnock, and two of Rob Roy's sons.

Attaching themselves mainly to the Duke of Perth's Regiment, they fought with bravery and distinction against the Hanoverian troops at the battle of Prestonpans.

Following the return of the Jacobite army to Scotland from England, a force of MacGregors was responsible for capturing Hanoverian troops and valuable supplies after a daring raid north of Inverness.

They only learned of the Jacobite defeat in the carnage of the battle of Culloden, fought on Drummossie Moor on April 16, after returning from this foray.

Chapter four:

For civil rights

While many Kings fought on the battlefield in the cause of freedom, others chose peaceful protest as their weapon.

Foremost among them was the charismatic civil rights leader Martin Luther King, whose assassination in 1968 stunned not only his fellow black Americans but the world at large.

Born in Atlanta, Georgia, in 1929, King was aged 24 when in 1953 he became pastor of the Dexter Avenue Baptist Church in Montgomery, Alabama.

He gained both a national and an international profile two years later when he led a boycott of buses in Montgomery, a boycott that began when Rosa Parks refused to obey a law that required her to surrender her seat to a white man.

The boycott lasted for more than a year, during which King's house was bombed and he was also arrested at one stage.

Victory was at last achieved, however, when the United States Supreme Court outlawed racial segregation on all intrastate buses.

Tirelessly active in the cause of human rights for his fellow black Americans, King founded the Southern Christian Leadership Conference (SCLC) in 1957, and this influential body co-ordinated the efforts of black church members throughout the racist southern states to conduct non-violent protests to win reform of civil rights.

Martin Luther King is perhaps most famously known for a speech he delivered in the front of the Lincoln memorial in March of 1963 during a march on Washington to call for jobs and freedom for oppressed black Americans.

Known as the '*I Have A Dream*' speech, its powerful message still resonates today.

Thanks to the efforts of King and the thousands of other civil rights campaigners drawn from all colours, classes, and creeds across America, a Civil Rights Act was passed in 1964, the same year that he was awarded the

Martin Luther King

Nobel Peace Prize. This was followed a year later by a Voting Rights Act.

On April 4, 1968, King visited Memphis, Tennessee, to give his support to striking sanitation workers. Shortly after 6pm, however, and to the world's horror, he was shot dead while standing on the balcony of the city's Lorraine Motel.

The assassination sparked off a wave of riots in more than sixty American cities, and calm was only restored four days later when President Lyndon Johnston declared a day of national of mourning and more than 300,000 people attended the murdered civil rights leader's funeral.

A lone gunman, James Earl Ray, was eventually found guilty of the murder, and sentenced to a 99-year prison term, but some conspiracy theorists disturbingly claim that he may not have acted alone.

Other Kings have found fame in the worlds of sport and literature.

On the tennis court, Billie Jean King, born in 1943 in Long Beach, California, is the name the now divorced Billie Jean Moffat took when she married law student Lawrence King in 1965.

Inducted into the International Tennis Hall of Fame in 1987, she won the first of her six titles at Wimbledon in 1966, a venue where she eventually amassed no less than a total of six singles titles, ten women's doubles titles, and four mixed doubles titles.

An advocate against sexism in both sport and society in general, she is also the proud holder of twelve Grand Slam single titles, fourteen Grand Slam women's doubles titles, and eleven Grand Slam mixed doubles titles.

In the world of music, Carole King is the singer and songwriter born in Brooklyn, New York, as Carole Klein, while Riley B. King, better known as B.B. King is the American blues guitarist born in Mississippi.

In the world of popular fiction, Stephen King is the best-selling author of horror fiction who was born at Portland, Maine, in 1947, and whose many works include *Carrie*, *Salem's Lot*, *The Shining*, and *The Stand*.